Islam

Major World Religions

Buddhism

Christianity

Hinduism

Islam

Judaism

Sikhism

Islam

Michael Ashkar

MASON CREST
PHILADELPHIA

Mason Crest
450 Parkway Drive, Suite D
Broomall, PA 19008
www.masoncrest.com

©2018 by Mason Crest, an imprint of National Highlights, Inc.

Printed and bound in the United States of America.

CPSIA Compliance Information: Batch #MWR2017.
For further information, contact Mason Crest at 1-866-MCP-Book.

3 5 7 9 8 6 4 2

Library of Congress Cataloging-in-Publication Data

on file at the Library of Congress
ISBN: 978-1-4222-3819-6 (hc)
ISBN: 978-1-4222-7972-4 (ebook)

Major World Religions series ISBN: 978-1-4222-3815-8

QR CODES AND LINKS TO THIRD-PARTY CONTENT

Table of Contents

1: What Do Muslims Believe? **9**

2: The Origins of Islam **21**

3: The Five Pillars of Islam **41**

4: How Muslims Worship **57**

5: Muslim Values in the Modern World **71**

Religious Demographics **92**

Quick Reference: Islam **95**

Islam Timeline **98**

Series Glossary of Key Terms **102**

Organizations to Contact **104**

Further Reading **105**

Internet Resources **106**

Index **108**

Photo Credits/About the Author **112**

KEY ICONS TO LOOK FOR:

Words to understand: These words with their easy-to-understand definitions will increase the reader's understanding of the text while building vocabulary skills.

Sidebars: This boxed material within the main text allows readers to build knowledge, gain insights, explore possibilities, and broaden their perspectives by weaving together additional information to provide realistic and holistic perspectives.

Educational Videos: Readers can view videos by scanning our QR codes, providing them with additional educational content to supplement the text. Examples include news coverage, moments in history, speeches, iconic sports moments and much more!

Text-dependent questions: These questions send the reader back to the text for more careful attention to the evidence presented there.

Research projects: Readers are pointed toward areas of further inquiry connected to each chapter. Suggestions are provided for projects that encourage deeper research and analysis.

Series glossary of key terms: This back-of-the book glossary contains terminology used throughout this series. Words found here increase the reader's ability to read and comprehend higher-level books and articles in this field.

A crowd of Muslim pilgrims walks around an ancient shrine in Mecca, Saudi Arabia, as part of a ritual that shows their submission to Allah.

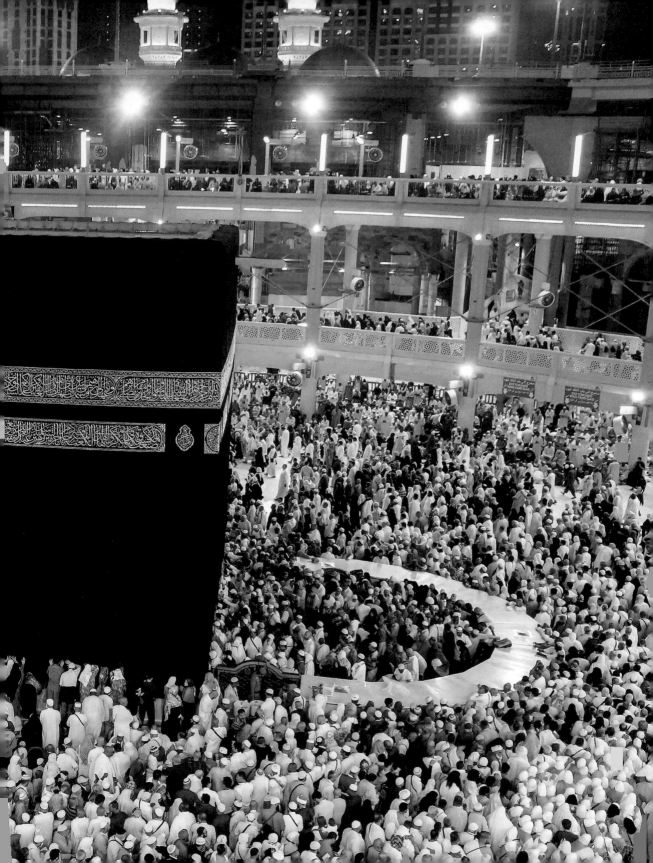

 Words to Understand in This Chapter

Allah—Arabic name used for God in Islam in preference to the word for "God"; has no plural and no gender-distinctive characteristics.

prophet—a man or woman who acts as a messenger from God.

Qur'an—the holy book of Islam, believed to contain Allah's actual words, as revealed to Muhammad.

Shi'a Islam—a Muslim sect whose members believe that Ali and his descendants were the legitimate successors to the Prophet Muhammad. Shiites, as they are known, make up between 15 and 20 percent of the total Muslim population.

Sunni Islam—the majority sect of Muslims, making up about 80 percent of the total population. Sunnis believe that they are following the proper path that was set out by Muhammad and the early Islamic community.

One meaning of the word Islam *is "peace," and Muslims greet each other with the words* Salaam aleikum *"Peace be with you." Islam teaches that people shall find peace with themselves and with each other through submission to the will of God.*

1 What Do Muslims Believe?

Nearly 2 billion people around the world live their lives following the beliefs and traditions of Islam. This religion originated in the seventh century CE on the Arabian Peninsula, but within a few centuries it had spread all over the world. Followers of Islam, who are called Muslims, believe in one God, whom they call *Allah*. They believe that a man named Muhammad was a *prophet* who brought Allah's messages to humankind.

The word *Islam* means "to surrender" or "to submit." People all submit themselves to others in some way. Children are expected to obey their parents and teachers; teachers obey the school principal; employees do what their employer requires them to do, and all citizens have to obey the laws of their homeland. Muslims believe that God is the highest authority of all, and that His teachings must be obeyed at all times. Obedience to the will of Allah comes before all other obligations.

The word *Islam* is also connected with the Arabic word for "peace." Muslims believe that obedience to God is the only way for people to find true fulfilment and peace with themselves.

The most important beliefs of Islam are summed up in the *Shahadah*, the Islamic declaration of faith. It states, in Arabic: "There is no god except Allah; Muhammad is the Messenger of Allah."

There are five articles of faith in Islam: belief in Allah, his angels, his Books, his Messengers, and Life after death. Muslims believe that nothing can be compared with God, but that there are other spiritual beings—the angels—that are heavenly servants of God. Everyone has two angels looking over their shoulders, to record their good and their bad deeds. To guide people, God sent his prophets, the most important of whom are the Messengers, who brought God's word in holy books.

Muslims believe this life is a preparation for the next. Their goal in life is to please God and, after death, to be rewarded in Heaven. They want to avoid displeasing God and being punished in Hell.

The Muslim Concept of God

Humans can never fully know or understand what God is like, Muslims believe. God is totally different from humans in many ways. He is eternal—without beginning and with-

Chinese Muslims pray in a mosque in Yinchuan.

out end. He is all-powerful, all-seeing, and all-knowing. For this reason, Muslims never try to depict God in statues or artwork. In fact, Islam forbids images of God, so that they can't be worshipped like pagan idols.

So how do Muslims know that God exists? They say he has revealed himself in certain ways. There is evidence in the order of the vast universe, and in the diversity of the world, and in the beauty and intricacy in each living thing. Looking at all this, Muslims see the only rational explanation as the Creator God.

Muslims learn about God from their holy book, the *Qur'an*, which, they believe, contains God's actual words. The Qur'an includes 99 "beautiful names" for God, such as "The Creator," "The Generous," and "The Guide."

Muslims look around at the magnificence of the natural world, filled with wonder at the power of Allah, whom they believe is the Creator of everything. They believe Allah has made them responsible for the Earth, and that they should care for the environment they live in.

A Global Religion

Islam is the second-biggest religion in the world, after Christianity. The Prophet Muhammad was an Arab, and the religion originated in the Arabian Peninsula. However, most Muslims today are not Arabs. Muslims live on all five inhabited continents, although most Muslims are found in Asia, Africa, and the region known as the Middle East. These were lands where Islam spread in the first few centuries after Muhammad's death.

Sometimes the Islamic religion was brought to new lands by conquering armies. Other times, it was introduced peacefully by traders and missionaries. This is how Islam arrived in east Africa and in the lands along the Indian Ocean. Today, south Asian countries are home to the largest populations of Muslims. In Indonesia, more

Educational Video

To hear the Muslim call to prayer, scan here.

than 205 million Indonesians are Muslims, while Pakistan is home to nearly 180 million Muslims. India has about 172 million Muslims, although this represents just about 14 percent of the country's total population. (Most Indians are Hindus.) Bangladesh is home to about 145 million Muslims.

The continent of Africa is home to nearly one-third of the total Muslim population. The largest Muslim population in Africa is found in Nigeria, in western Africa, where

Some countries in Asia, such as Iran, Turkey, Indonesia, and Pakistan, and most countries in the Middle East have populations that are more than 90 percent Muslim.

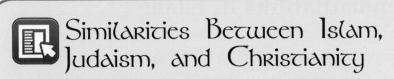 Similarities Between Islam, Judaism, and Christianity

- All three religions originated in the Middle East.
- They are all monotheistic, believing in one God. Muslims claim that their God (Allah) is the same as the one worshipped by Jews and Christians. However, many Jews and Christians disagree with this interpretation.
- All three religions share certain traditions, going back to the time of Ibrahim (or Abraham).
- Followers of all three religions believe that God's Word is revealed in their holy scriptures. Christians believe in the teaching of the Jewish Bible (which Christians call the Old Testament), but claim that the message of Jesus (recorded in the New Testament) has replaced some of the ancient Jewish laws. Muslims believe that both the Jewish and Christian scriptures are sacred, but that the revelations contains in the Qur'an supersedes those earlier writings.
- All three are ethical religions, concerned to ensure that their followers should lead morally upright lives, in accordance with the will of God.

more than 93 million Muslims live. Egypt is home to more than 80 million Muslims. It is located in North Africa, and in Egypt and other countries in this region—including Algeria, Morocco, and Libya—more than 95 percent of the population follows Islam.

Denominations in Islam

Like other religions, Islam has its different branches. About 80 percent of Muslims follow a branch known as *Sunni Islam*. (The word *Sunni* comes from an Arabic term meaning "path.") Sunni Muslims believe that they follow the right path of Islam. This main branch of Islam has dominated the religion almost continuously since 661. Between 15 and 20 percent of Muslims follow a minority branch known as *Shi'a Islam*. They are known as Shiites.

Muslim students read the Arabic Qur'an, so they can learn to recite it by heart. Someone who can recite the entire Qur'an is called a Hafiz.

Shiites pray during a ceremony in Pakistan. The Shiites are a minority sect within Islam, making up about 15 to 20 percent of the total Muslim population. In recent years tensions between the Sunni and Shiite communities have risen, with each side believing that it is following the true path set by the Prophet Muhammad.

These two sects originated around the time of Muhammad's death. The Shiites disagreed with the Sunnis over who should succeed Muhammad as the leader of the faithful on earth. Shiites believed that Muhammad's son-in-law, a man named Ali ibn Abi Talib, should be Muhammad's successor. (The word *Shia* means "party," and became the name for those who belonged to the "party of Ali.")

Shiites do not recognize the Sunni caliphs who were chosen as Muslim leaders over the next few centuries.

Sufi Prayer

The Naqshabandi order of Sufis was begun in the fourteenth century and still exists today. It was named after its founder, who wrote these lines (here paraphrased) as part of a prayer:

O my God, how gentle are you with him who has transgressed against you: how near are you to him who seeks you, how tender to him who petitions you, how kindly to him who hopes in you.

Instead, they revere their own line of leaders, called Imams, all of whom were descendants of Muhammad and Ali. The Shi'a are themselves divided into numerous subgroups, such as the Twelvers, who believe that there were twelve Imams, and Seveners, who say that there were only seven. Most Shi'a Muslims belong to the Twelver sect. Shia Islam is the official religion in Iran, and Shiite Muslims form the largest religious group in Iraq and Bahrain. There are significant numbers of Shiites in Lebanon, Syria, Saudi Arabia, Pakistan, Afghanistan, Azerbaijan, Yemen, and India.

Today, both Shiites and Sunnis argue that their way is the correct one prescribed by the Prophet Muhammad, and that the other group has been misled by false teachers. Tensions between Sunnis and Shiites in the Middle East have been high for decades, with major conflicts between the two groups in places like Iraq, Lebanon, and Yemen.

Other sects of Islam include the Ibadiyyah, the Druze, and the Zaidis. They are very small sects, making up just a small proportion of the total Muslim population.

Members of any Muslim sect can participate in the practices of Sufism. This is a mystical element of Islam that includes the belief that through prayer and meditation, a Muslim can experience direct union with Allah. Sufi beliefs emphasize the love and mercy of Allah. Dance, poetry, and music help Sufis reach an ecstatic state that they feel brings their spirits closer to Allah.

Despite the religions differences of these sects, all Muslims may worship together and may intermarry.

 ## Text-Dependent Questions

1. What is the Shahadah?
2. What is the name of the Muslim holy book?

 ## Research Project

The CIA World Factbook website (https://www.cia.gov/library/publications/the-world-factbook) has population and religious adherence figures for all nations. Print out a large map of the world, and note the number of Muslims living in each country. What countries have the largest number of Muslims? Why? Do research in your school library or the Internet to support your conclusions.

 ## Words to Understand in This Chapter

Hadith—saying, report, account—the sayings of the Prophet Muhammad, as recounted by his household, descendants, and companions.

revelation—knowledge that is revealed to a person by God.

The Prophet Muhammad was a trader who traveled throughout the Arabian peninsula with camel caravans. As a result he was exposed to the religious ideas of many groups of people, including Christians and Jews.

2 The Origins of Islam

historians say that the Prophet Muhammad started the religion of Islam in the seventh century. Muslims prefer to say that Allah is the founder and that Adam, the very first man, was also the first Muslim because he "surrendered" himself to God.

Muhammad was born in about 570 CE in Arabia, in the city of Mecca. At the time, this was a trading center for the tribes of the Arabian Peninsula, as well as a religious center. At the time, most people of the region were pagans. They worshipped many gods, who were represented by idols of various shapes and sizes. In Mecca there was a shrine that people traveled to, where they could worship their favorite idols.

Muhammad became a trader, traveling across the deserts of the Arabian Peninsula with caravans carrying goods from place to place. During his travels, he often came into contact with people who followed a variety of religious beliefs, such as Jews and Christians. Muhammad was a good man, who became known as al-Amin, meaning "The Trustworthy." Muhammad rejected the worship of idols that took place in Mecca. In time he came to believe that there was only one God, Allah. When he was not working, he would sometimes go to a cave on a hillside near the city, where he would spend time alone in prayer.

One night (later named the "Night of Power"), Muhammad was in the cave when he had a terrifying experience. Muslims say that the angel Jibreel (or Gabriel) came to him and ordered him to "read" or "recite" (the two words are the same in Arabic.) Muhammad was illiterate and could not read, but eventually he realized that he was being told to remember the words of the angel and recite them to the people. This first visit, or *revelation*, happened when Muhammad was about 40 years of age, around the year 610 CE. Many other revelations followed.

Muhammad passed these divine messages on to his followers, who wrote them down many years after his death. Muslims believe that the messages from the angel are the word of Allah. The messages are preserved in the Qur'an, which is Arabic for "recitation." That fateful night changed Muhammad's life and the course of history.

The Origins of Islam

Muhammad did not immediately begin sharing the revelations from Allah. He was scared, so at first he discussed it

Messengers of God

A prophet is someone through whom God speaks. Islam recognizes thousands of prophets, because Muslims believe that God has spoken through many people during different ages and in different parts of the world. However, just twenty-five prophets are named in the Qur'an. Most of them are figures who are also considered prophets by followers of Judaism and Christianity, and are mentioned in the scriptures of those religions. Some of their names are slightly different in Arabic. For example, Abraham—an important figure in the Jewish religion—is called Ibrahim by Muslims. Joseph, who saved the forebears of the Jews from a famine, is called Yusuf.

Muslims believe that five major prophets lived before Muhammad. In chronological order, they were Adam, the first man; Nuh (Noah), who built the ark that survived the Great Flood; Ibrahim; Musa (Moses); and Isa (Jesus). Muslims believe that all of these prophets were inspired by God and taught the same basic truth, but that God's message became corrupted over time. Muhammad is called the "Seal of the Prophets," because Muslims believe he is the final prophet sent by God. The teachings that Muhammad revealed in the Qur'an, Muslims say, is the final revelation of God for all humankind and for all time. It is the complete and unaltered Word of God, and so there is no need of further prophets after Muhammad.

The most important prophets are the Messengers, who set down the Word of God in holy books. For instance, Moses and the Torah; Jesus and the Gospels; and Muhammad and the Qur'an.

only with his wife, Kadijah. Then he told a few close friends, including his nephew Ali. It was a few years before Muhammad felt ready to begin preaching publicly in Mecca. He told the people that there was only one God, Allah. He also spoke out against injustice and cruel practices that were common in the society of Mecca at the time.

Because Mecca was the center of religion on the Arabian Peninsula, where people came to worship idols, the religious leaders of the city were not happy about Muhammad's message. They plotted against him, and tried to have him killed. They also attacked those who followed Muhammad, or refused to give them jobs or to do business with the early Muslims. But Muhammad would not stop preaching the message he had received from Allah. The persecution grew so bad that in 622, Muhammad and about 200 of his followers left Mecca.

Today, it seems obvious that if a person is being persecuted for his or her beliefs, that person should find a safe place elsewhere. However, leaving Mecca was a major step for Muhammad. According to the Arab society of the time, this move meant that Muhammad had abandoned his tribe and he deserved to be punished by death.

Muhammad and his followers settled in a small town called Medina, which is about 275 miles (440 km) away. There, Muhammad set up the first Islamic state, run by religious laws.

Over the next few years, the Arabs of Mecca fought with Muhammad and his followers in Medina. Both sides won and lost battles, but Muhammad was successful at

This painting from Turkey depicts the Prophet Muhammad (in green) praying with his nephew Ali and his wife Kadijah. Most depictions of Muhammad do not show his face; since around 1500 it is relatively rare for the prophet to be pictured in artwork at all.

"If there are any among you who worshiped Muhammad, he is dead. But if it is Allah you worship, He lives forever."

When Muhammad died, he did not name anyone to succeed him as leader of the Muslims. So the members of the Muslim community had to choose a caliph, or "successor," to the Prophet. Even though they ruled a large area, the caliphs did not call themselves "kings" or "emperors," because they considered themselves to be rulers under Allah, the supreme king. The territories that they ruled became known as the caliphate.

After Muhammad's death, some people in Medina thought his cousin Ali ibn Abi Talib should become the caliph. Although Ali was much younger than Muhammad, there was a close friendship between them. Ali was one of the first people to convert to Islam, along with Muhammad's first wife Kadijah. He had also been one of the bravest fighters in the war against Mecca, and had married Muhammad's daughter Fatima.

However, the Muslim community chose another of Muhammad's closest companions, Abu Bakr, to be the first caliph. Abu Bakr had been an early convert to Islam, and was widely respected for his religious devotion. The tribal unity Islam had fostered on the Arabian Peninsula threatened to deteriorate after Muhammad's death, and Abu Bakr worked to consolidate the support of the Arab tribes before his own death just two years later, in 634.

The next caliph was Umar, who like Ali and Abu Bakr was a member of the same tribe as Muhammad, the Quraysh. Umar ruled for a decade, from 634 to 644. During

According to Muslim tradition, the Prophet Muhammad is buried beneath the green dome of this mosque in the city of Medina, in present-day Saudi Arabia.

his time as caliph, Islam expanded both east and west. Umar maintained a large military, and his forces captured territory from the Persian Empire, as well as Syria and Egypt, which at the time were provinces of the Byzantine (Roman) Empire. Followers of pagan religions who lived in the conquered territories were ordered to convert to Islam or they would be killed. Most of the people converted to Islam. The Muslims did allow Christians and Jews to live without renouncing their faiths if they wished, but those who did so had to swear allegiance to the Muslim state and pay extra taxes. Some Christians and Jews refused to give up their faiths and paid the tax; others decided to convert because of the benefits they would receive as Muslims in the growing Islamic empire.

After Umar died, another of Muhammad's closest companions, Uthman, was chosen as the third caliph. During Uthman's rule from 644 to 656, the Arabs continued to conquer territories. Uthman also oversaw a major accomplishment, as the first official text of the Qur'an was compiled under his leadership. (Prior to this, the revelations of Allah had been memorized and repeated by the Muslim community, rather than being written down.) However, Uthman was not as skillful or popular a political leader as the two previous caliphs had been. This led to a revolt among the Muslims. In 656, Uthman was murdered.

After Uthman died, Muhammad's cousin Ali finally became caliph. For many years, a group of Muslims had supported Ali. They believed that only members of Muhammad's family should be given the position of leader of Islam, and that as Muhammad's son-in-law Ali was the logical choice. These supporters came to be commonly known as the Shiites (from *shiat Ali*, Arabic for "party of Ali").

Ali had not been involved in the plot to kill Uthman—in fact, two of his sons had been among the caliph's guards. However, the divisions within the Muslim community did not disappear with Uthman's death, and a civil war soon began. Abu Bakr's daughter Aisha, who had been Muhammad's youngest wife, and Uthman's nephew

Copies of the Qur'an are often decorated with beautiful geometric patterns. The harmony of these intricate designs reflects the order and balance of God's created universe.

Muawiya, the governor of Syria, both challenged Ali for power.

Ali did not want Muslims to fight other Muslims. After capturing Aisha in a battle, he treated her with respect and allowed her to go home. During another battle, he ordered his army to stop fighting, even though they were winning, because Muawiya's soldiers had placed passages from the Qur'an onto the ends of their spears. Ali tried to compromise with Muawiya, but this offended a small group of his

This Persian painting shows the forces of the caliph Ali battling against the army of Muawiya, governor of Syria. After Ali was assassinated, Muawiya seized control over the Muslim empire.

own supporters. This group came to be known as the Kharijis ("seceders"). Although Ali's forces defeated the Kharijis in a decisive battle, one of them murdered Ali in 661.

Changes in Leadership

The death of Ali ended what would become known as the era of the four "rightly guided caliphs." These companions of the Prophet Muhammad had guided the expansion of the Muslim empire for about 30 years. The four "rightly guided" caliphs lived humble lives and were in close touch with the people. But the Muslim rulers who followed them became corrupted by wealth and power. They were no longer elected on the strength of their character, but inherited the position from their fathers.

After Ali's death Muawiya declared himself caliph and inaugurated the Umayyad dynasty, which was to last almost a century. Ali's supporters urged his sons to seek the leadership, but Ali's oldest son Hassan agreed not to pursue his claim to the position of caliph. Hassan died soon after, allegedly poisoned by his enemies. Ali's younger son Hussein also agreed not to vie for the position of caliph until Muawiya died. However, while he was still alive Muawiya declared that his son Yazid would succeed him as caliph, therefore substituting a hereditary line of rule for the previously established system of electing the most qualified leader. Hussein's followers declared war against Yazid, but they were vastly outnumbered and were defeated at the Battle of Karbala in 680. Hussein and most of his family were killed when he refused to surrender his claim to the caliphate. His infant son Ali survived, however, so the Shiite line of leadership continued.

The Spread of Islam Continues

During the rule of the four "rightly guided caliphs," Islam spread far beyond the Arabian Peninsula. Muslim armies captured territory to the northeast, into Syria and Persia (Iran), and to the northwest along the Mediterranean coast of Africa, into Egypt and Libya. A hundred years after Muhammad's death, Islam had spread through all the North African countries, into Spain in Europe, and had reached as far eastward as India.

The rapid growth of Islam was not without problems. Expansion into new lands meant that the Islamic world encompassed a wide variety of tribal and cultural practices. For the first time, many Arabs were exposed to the philosophical thought of the ancient Greeks, Romans, and Persians. Some Muslims, influenced by these older cultures, attempted to introduce new doctrines into Islam. Over the next few centuries, Sunni Muslim scholars attempted to establish laws and religious practices that would keep Muslims following the path set by Muhammad and the Qur'an.

Division of the Islamic Empire

During the first decades of rule by the Umayyad caliphs, the Islamic world was divided by civil wars as various factions fought for power. Muhammad and the first four caliphs had

This mosque, known as the Dome of the Rock, was built in Jerusalem by the Umayyad caliph in 691 ce. It is located on the foundation of the ancient Jewish temple, and is one of the oldest existing examples of Islamic architecture.

ruled from Medina, and had lived simply as an example to other Muslims. The Umayyad caliphs, by contrast, moved the capital of the Islamic state to Damascus, where many of their supporters lived. The Umayyads enjoyed their wealth and wanted to be treated like royalty. Their lavish excesses angered many pious Muslims, and Umayyad caliphs often had to put down revolts in order to keep their power.

During this period Islam did not spread only through conquest; the number of believers also continued to grow through conversion by more peaceful means. Traders or

Muslims pray at Juma Masjid, a mosque in India. Islam reached India in about 750.

missionaries, rather than soldiers, first exposed many people to the tenets of Islam, particularly in Asia. The exchange of ideas through contact with other cultures helped Islam to develop and, in many ways, shaped the direction of the Islamic state.

The Umayyad caliphs were ultimately overthrown in a civil war, and a new family, the Abbasids, took power over the Islamic state in 750. They reigned for five centuries, during which the Islamic state reached its greatest glory. At a time that Christian Europe was stagnating in the "Dark Ages," the Islamic empire was a global center of knowledge and learning. Muslim scholars made great discoveries in mathematics, natural sciences, medicine, fine arts, architecture, philosophy, astronomy, and geography.

Educational Video

Click here for a film about the Sunni-Shia division.

However, the Abbasids found it difficult to control their vast empire, which was based in their stronghold in Baghdad. Facing revolts and civil wars, they gradually allowed various regions to withdraw and form self-governing kingdoms. Some of these kingdoms paid monetary tribute to the Abbasids, while others became completely independent. Independent Muslim kingdoms emerged in Iran, Arabia, North Africa, Turkey, Spain, and northern India. By the tenth century, the Abbasid caliph in Baghdad was merely a figurehead who symbolized Muslim unity, rather than a strong political leader, even though the caliph still controlled parts of the once-vast empire.

The Islamic world would also face challenges from outside its borders. Between 1095 and 1291, Muslims in the Middle East fought a series of wars against Christian armies from Europe. These conflicts, known as the Crusades, were for control over Jersualem and other areas that both Christians and Muslims considered sacred. In the

From 1483 until 1924 the Ottoman Empire was the most powerful Islamic state in the world. It threatened to conquer Christian Europe in the sixteenth and seventeenth centuries, before being defeated at the Battle of Vienna in 1683. The Ottoman ruler, known as the sultan, was considered to be the spiritual leader of Sunni Muslims.

1250s, a new threat to the Abbasids emerged from the East. Horsemen from China known as the Mongols, led by Genghis Khan, conquered most of Asia. In 1258 they sacked the city of Baghdad, bringing the power of the Abbasid caliphate to an end.

Though it was no longer appropriate to speak of a united Muslim empire, there was no denying the existence of a Muslim world. A large portion of the global population was firmly committed to the religion that had emerged out of the deserts of Arabia just a few centuries earlier. Even the Mongols were eventually converted to Islam. Smaller Muslim kingdoms were established, along with the powerful Ottoman Empire, based in Turkey. Throughout all of Muslim history, however, Mecca remained the religious center of Islam, and is so today.

 Text-Dependent Questions

1. When did Muhammad receive his first revelation from Allah?
2. In what year did the Muslims under Muhammad conquer Mecca?
3. Which city did the Abbasid rulers make the capital of the Islamic empire after gaining control from the Umayyad dynasty in 750 CE?

 Research Project

Using the Internet or your school library, research the life of an important figure from the early days of Islam, such as the Prophet Muhammad or one of the rightly guided caliphs. Write a two page report about this person and present it to your class.

 ## Words to Understand in This Chapter

Hajj—annual pilgrimage to Mecca, which each Muslim must undertake at least once in a lifetime if he or she is fit enough and can afford to do so.

halal—anything that is permitted or lawful in Islam.

Hijrah—departure, exit, emigration—the emigration of the Prophet Muhammad from Mecca to Medina in 622 CE; the event that starts the Islamic calendar.

Ramadan—ninth month of the Islamic calendar, when fasting is required from just before dawn until sunset, as ordered by Allah in the Qur'an.

salah—five different prayers, recited every day in Arabic, in the manner taught by the Prophet Muhammad, spread at intervals from first thing in the morning until last thing at night.

sawm—fasting from just before dawn until sunset; abstinence from all food and drink (including water), as well as smoking and sex.

zakah—purification of wealth by payment of an annual welfare due—an obligatory act of worship.

Every day is regulated by prayer, even when Muslims are not in the most convenient place to pray. In Muslim countries, it is not unusual to see Muslims praying in the streets or in open areas.

3 The Five Pillars of Islam

There are five duties that adult Muslims are expected to follow, known as the Five Pillars of Islam. Just as pillars help to hold up a building, so these Five Pillars are meant to help Muslims worship Allah properly and lead good lives.

Unlike most other religions, Islam has no coming-of-age ceremony, when believers promise to keep the rules of their religion. Muslim children gradually learn their beliefs and practices as they grow up in a Muslim home, going to the mosque with their parents, and attending the mosque school in the evenings or at weekends. In some Muslim communities, children are expected, once they reach the age of ten, to take on the obligations of the Five Pillars for themselves. In other communities, puberty is seen as the point at which they become adults and accept these responsibilities.

The first pillar is *Shahadah*—the declaration of belief in Allah as the only God, and of belief in Muhammad as the Messenger of God. This statement of belief affects the whole of a Muslim's life.

Salah, or ritual prayer, is the second pillar. There are five daily prayers, spread at intervals from early in the morning until late at night.

Fasting, called *sawm*, is the third pillar. Muslims fast every year for the whole of the Muslim month called *Ramadan*.

The fourth pillar is *zakah*—the charity tax—which is usually paid annually. Muslims are required to give a small portion of their wealth to support the needy.

The great pilgrimage, called *Hajj*, is the fifth pillar. Every Muslim wants to make a pilgrimage, or journey, to Mecca at least once in their lifetime. But only about 10 percent of all Muslims accomplish this, as many are too poor. While in Mecca the pilgrims participate in many activities and rituals that are meant to show the unity of the Muslim community.

When Do Muslims Fast?

Muslims fast during the daylight hours of the month of Ramadan (the ninth month in the Islamic calendar). They must go without food or drink, and abstain from smoking or sex during this time. They should also avoid any bad thoughts, words, or deeds.

Muhammad and the Five Pillars

In 632 CE, Muhammad preached his famous Farewell Speech while on pilgrimage to Mecca. He urged Muslims to keep their religion. In his speech, he referred to the Five Pillars: "O People, listen to me in earnest: worship Allah, say your five daily prayers, fast during Ramadan, give your wealth in Zakah, and perform Hajj if you can afford it." A few months later, Muhammad died and was buried in his hometown of Medina.

All Muslims must fast, except for those who are weak due to disease or illness and those who need to keep up their strength. Young children and the elderly would not be expected to fast, nor would sick people, pregnant women, nursing mothers, soldiers, or travelers. However, most Muslims fast if they can.

The practice of fasting is laid down in the Qur'an. It also says there that Muhammad began to receive the revelations of the Qur'an during Ramadan, making it an especially holy month. When Muslims fast, they are giving up something for God, so fasting is an expression of their faith in God.

Fasting has other purposes too. It allows Muslims to experience hunger, making them more able to sympathize with the poor, who often go hungry. It tests their powers of endurance, so that they will be strong enough to cope with whatever life has in store. It helps them learn self-control, making them less selfish and more able to resist evil.

Why Do Muslims Give to Charity?

Islam encourages people to work hard and be generous to others. Muslims are expected to give at least 2.5 percent of their wealth to those in need. In some Muslim countries this is collected, like income tax. In others, it is left to the individual to decide to support a Muslim charity, such as Muslim Aid. Muslims who work in other countries often send money home to help their community.

The word *Zakah* means "purification." Giving away a percentage of your wealth, Muslims believe, purifies the

During Ramadan, Muslims go about their daily work and duties almost as normal. In the evening, they will shop for the evening meal (iftar) that they will eat after sunset. People gather together and enjoy these meals after a long day of fasting. These Muslims are enjoying their iftar meal on the streets of Sarajevo, Bosnia and Herzegovina.

rest for your own use. If God blesses your labors with rewards, Muslims believe, you should thank God and enjoy your wealth, sharing your blessings with others.

Rites of Passage

Islam has few rites of passage, the most important ones being at birth and death. Most others are cultural rather than religious ceremonies and differ from one country to another.

The birth of a new baby is a cause for much celebration in Islam. Every child is a gift and blessing from God. When the baby is seven days old, the *aqiqah* ceremony takes place. The baby's hair is shaved off and weighed, and the same weight in gold or silver is given to the poor. Even if the baby is bald, a donation is still made. To give thanks for the child, two sheep or goats are killed for a feast if it is a boy, or one for a girl. The meat is shared with the family and visitors, and a third of it is given to the poor.

Circumcision—the removal of the foreskin from the male penis—is widely practiced in the Islamic world. In fact, Muslims are the largest religious group in which this practice is widespread. It is considered a sign of belonging to the wider Islamic community. In some Muslim cultures, particularly in Africa and Malaysia, females are "circumcised" as well—a barbaric practice known as "female genital mutilation," that is condemned by many people in the Western world.

Although Muslim boys are often circumcised during the *aqiqah* ceremony, this can vary from region to region. For example, in Turkey boys are circumcised between the ages of seven and ten, and this is treated as their initiation into manhood.

By the age of four, Muslim children are expected to be able to say the Arabic phrase *Bismillah-ir-Rahman-ir-Rahim*, meaning "In the name of God, the Merciful, the Compassionate." This is the opening of almost every chapter of the Qur'an, and the words are frequently spoken by Muslims. Learning to say this marks the beginning of a child's Islamic education, after which he or she will be taught to pray.

The most popular name for a boy is Muhammad, after the Prophet. Many other boys' names start with "Abd," meaning servant, such as Abdullah ("servant of God") or Abdul Rahman ("servant of the Merciful," another name for God). A girl might be named Ayesha (after one of Muhammad's wives) or Fatimah (his daughter).

Rituals for Death and Mourning

When a Muslim dies, the body is washed, wrapped in a shroud with the face uncovered, and buried as soon as possible, out of respect for the dead person. Cremation is forbidden by Islam because it is believed that the body will be raised up at the Last Day. The funeral service is simple, and often attended only by men. Those present at the graveside say a funeral prayer, asking Allah to forgive the dead person's sins so that he or she will go to heaven. The body is laid in a grave with the head turned to the right, facing Mecca, the direction of prayer.

During the aqiqah *ceremony, the call to prayer is whispered in the baby's ear, beginning with: "Allah is great I bear witness that Muhammad is the Messenger of Allah."*

Muslims do not encourage mourning or any elaborate ceremonies when someone dies. They have a strong belief in an afterlife and in the mercy of God for believers. It is important to them that they show acceptance of God's will over life and death.

The Islamic Calendar

When it comes to religious festivals, Muslims follow a different calendar than most people living in the Western world do. The Islamic calendar is based on the cycles of the moon,

When Muslims speak the name of Muhammad, or the name of some other prophet, they often say (in Arabic) "Peace be upon him," as a mark of respect. In English texts, this is sometimes indicated by PBUH.

whereas the Western calendar is based on the earth's rotation around the sun. Both the Islamic and Western calendars are divided into twelve months. However, in the Islamic calendar the length of months is based on the intervals between new moons, so months alternate between 29 and 30 days in length. A lunar year has either 355 or 354 days, so it is 10 or 11 days shorter than the solar year of 365 days.

A new month traditionally begins with the first sighting of the new crescent moon. (For centuries Muslims have been mathematically calculating the beginning of each month and creating their calendars on the basis of these calculations.) The twelve months of the Islamic calendar are Muharram, Safar, Rabia Awwal, Rabia Thani, Jumada Awwal, Jumada Thani, Rajab, Shaban, Ramadan, Shawwal, Dhu al-Qida, and Dhu al-Hijja.

The first day of Muharram is considered New Year's Day. It commemorates the day known as the *Hijrah*, or "emigration," when Muhammad and his followers left Mecca and settled in Medina. Muslim years are counted

Muslim festivals are religious occasions—opportunities to praise God, to remember the poor, and to gather together, encouraging each other in the faith.

from this event, which occurred in 622 CE. The year 2017 CE was the year 1439 AH in the Muslim calendar. (AH is an abbreviation for the Latin phrase *Anno Hegirae*, meaning "year of the hijrah").

Festivals and Celebrations

Compared with other religions, there are relatively few festivals in Islam. The two major ones, which all Muslims celebrate, are Eid al-Adha ("The Great Festival,") the festival of sacrifice at the end of Hajj; and Eid al-Fitr ("The Little

Eid al-Adha is the Festival of Sacrifice, when animals like this cow are killed for food. Families offer their best animal, to give thanks to God.

Festival,") the festival of fast-breaking at the end of Ramadan. Besides these, there are several other important days in the Muslim calendar. In Muslim countries, Eid al-Fitr is celebrated with a national holiday that can last for up to four days.

Educational Video

Scan here to learn 10 important facts about Ramadan.

Eid al-Fitr is the day of rejoicing at the end of Ramadan, when the long month of fasting is over. It takes place on the first of Shawwal, which is signified by the sighting of the new moon. In Muslim countries, there is a national holiday of up to four days. In western countries, many Muslims take the day off from work or school.

Children especially enjoy the festival, because they receive presents such as sweets, money, and new clothes. Families clean their homes and decorate them with greetings cards. They also invite relatives and friends to their homes to share their food.

The day begins with a visit to the mosque. So many families attend that it is often necessary to have several morning prayer-sessions, or to create more space by laying down sheets outside the mosque where people can pray. Birthdays that fall during the month of Ramadan are celebrated at Eid al-Fitr, and many weddings take place then, too. Families also remember their deceased relatives, and visit their graves at this time.

The fast during Ramadan helps Muslims to sympathize with people who go hungry, so Eid al-Fitr is also an occasion for sharing with the poor, and is sometimes called the Festival of Charity. Every Muslim who can afford it donates the cost of a meal. The money is often collected beforehand so that it can be distributed in time for the poor to enjoy the festival.

Many Muslims like to eat meat at festival times, even if they are too poor to do so regularly at other times. When Muslims kill an animal for food, they "sacrifice" it, as part of their religion, to remind themselves that they are taking a life and to thank God for his gift of life.

At Eid al-Adha, Muslim families sacrifice an animal at the same time that pilgrims on the Hajj to Mecca are doing the same. A family might offer a goat or sheep; a larger group could offer a camel or a cow. The festival is a time to eat well with family and friends, but also to remember the poor, who receive a third of the meat.

The Muslim method of sacrificing an animal is to slit its throat, while saying the Bismillah prayer. Only then is the meat considered to be *halal*, or "permitted." There is much controversy in Western countries over the ritual slaughter of animals. Scientists cannot agree on which method of slaughter causes the animal the least pain and trauma. Muslims believe that their method is the least painful way for the animal to die, particularly if it is killed at home, and spared the trauma of a journey to the abattoir.

There are several other important days that are observed in the Islamic lunar calendar. Although these festivals fall on the same date each year in the Muslim calendar, they are on different dates each year according to the Western calendar because of the ten or eleven day difference in the length of the lunar and solar years. So Muslim festivals can fall in different seasons.

Many Muslims will eat dates when breaking their Ramadan fast in the evening, because dates were a favorite food of the Prophet Muhammad.

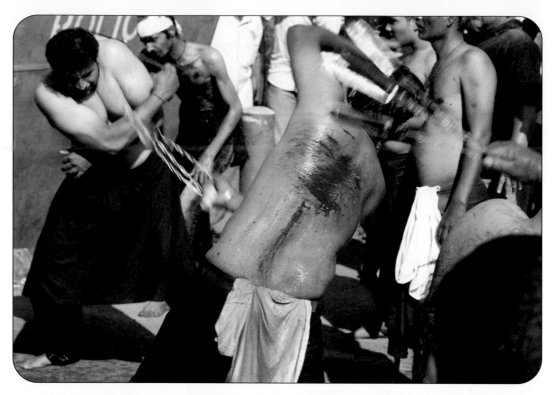

Some Shiite Muslims observe Ashura by self-flagellation—hitting themselves with whips or chains to commemorate the martyrdom of Imam Hussein in 680 CE.

Ashura, which falls on the ninth and tenth days of Muharram, is observed by Shi'ite Muslims as a day of fasting and mourning for the death in battle of the Prophet's grandson, Hussein.

The 12th of Rabi al-Awwal is Maulid ul Nabi—the Prophet's birthday. There are processions and people listen to stories about Muhammad's life.

The 27th of Rajab is Lailat-ul-Isra'wal Miraj, commemorating the miraculous Night Journey of Muhammad from Mecca to Jerusalem, and his ascension into heaven and return. Extra prayers are said that night.

The night of the 14–15th of Shaban is Lailat-ul-Barat, the Night of Forgiveness. Muslims believe that on this night, God decides what will happen to each person in the coming year. It is a time to repent of your sins and ask God for forgiveness. Many Muslims will stay awake all night, reading the Qur'an.

Lailat-ul-Qadr, on the 27th of Ramadan, honors the Night of Power, when Muhammad is said to have received his first revelation of the Qur'an. Many Muslims spend all night at a mosque, reading the Qur'an and praying.

 Text-Dependent Questions

1. When does the *aqiqah* ceremony take place? What occurrs at this ceremony?
2. How much shorter is the Islamic lunar calendar than the standard solar year of 365 days?

 Research Project

Using your school library or the internet, research the question, "Should you give to charity?" One perspective is that the world is unfair—the three wealthiest people in the world have more money than the 48 poorest countries combined, and millions of children die each year from poverty-related illnesses. So those who have more than they need should help those who lack enough resources to meet even basic needs. On the other hand, people deserve the money they have earned and should be able to spend it as they wish. Some people feel that charity demeans people and makes them dependent on others. Present your conclusion in a two-page report, providing examples from your research that support your answer.

 ## Words to Understand in This Chapter

ihram—state or condition entered into to perform Hajj; also, the name given to the two plain white unsewn clothes worn by male pilgrims, or to the modest clothing worn by women pilgrims.

jumu'ah—weekly communal *salah* (prayer), and attendance at the *khutbah* (speech) performed shortly after midday on Fridays.

Ka'bah—a cube-shaped structure in the center of the grand mosque in Mecca; believed by Muslims to be the original house built for the worship of the One True God.

masjid—a place of worship; a mosque.

minbar—a small set of steps in a mosque from which a sermon is given.

Muslims prostrating themselves in prayer before God. Prostration is not the most modest position, which is one reason why men and women pray separately and must dress modestly for community prayer.

4 How Muslims Worship

The whole of a Muslim's life is worship. The five main duties—the Five Pillars—are all ways of worshiping Allah. Muslims pray five times a day, as set down in the Pillar known in Arabic as *salah*.

Muslims prefer to recite prayers together with other Muslims whenever possible. The main act of worship of the week, called *jumu'ah*, takes place shortly after midday on Fridays. This includes a sermon from the imam, who leads the prayers. Muslims also say their own private prayers during salah.

Being clean in the presence of someone important is a mark of respect. Muslims pay God respect by washing before they pray, as God is the most important being in their lives. Washing also has a practical purpose. It is refreshing and helps the person who is praying to concentrate. Islam originated on the Arabian Peninsula, a hot, desert region; and many Muslims still live in hot countries today. Washing also reminds Muslims of prayer, because they can apologize to God for sins, and wash them away.

There is a special way that Muslims wash before prayer. It is called **wudu** in Arabic. First, they wash their hands thoroughly, then their mouths, nostrils, and faces, three times. Next, they wash their arms three times. They run wet hands over their head, wiping their neck and their ears. Lastly, they wash their feet thoroughly up to the ankle, starting with the right foot.

The Purpose of Prayer

Prayer is an important element in all religions. It can take different forms. Prayer can be a way of speaking to God, or of listening to God in silence. People of all ages can find prayer very satisfying. They can use it to ask God for forgiveness when they feel guilty; they use it to praise God and to thank God for all the blessings in their lives; and they can pray for other people as well as for themselves.

There is a series of movements that Muslims make when they pray. It is called a *rak'ah* in Arabic. Different prayer sessions have two, three, or four *rak'ahs*. A *rak'ah* consists of standing, bowing, and two prostrations, while reciting prayers and passages from the Qur'an.

Standing and bowing show respect to God. Prostration shows more because, if you kneel down on the floor with your forehead touching the ground, you are completely

When Muslims pray together, they line up together from the front, standing shoulder to shoulder. This is a sign of their unity and equality before God—no one is so important that they should stand apart from the rest.

helpless. It is a sign of submission. Muslims do this to show that they are entirely at the mercy of God. Prostration is the most important of the prayer positions: it shows what "Islam" means—"submission" to Allah. Muslims are people who submit themselves and their whole lives to God.

Muslims finish their prayers by sitting back on their heels and turning their heads to the right and then to the left, saying "Peace be on you, and Allah's blessings." This shows their concern for the people next to them, and by extension, for all of their Muslim brothers and sisters throughout the world.

Where do Muslims worship?

Muslims can worship God anywhere, as long as it is a clean place for them to put their forehead down on the ground in prostration. They often use prayer mats for this purpose. A place of prostration is called a mosque, or *masjid* in Arabic. We tend to think of mosques as special buildings, with domes and tall towers. But many mosques in hot countries are simply courtyards where Muslims can line up together in prayer. There must be somewhere for them to wash and somewhere to put their shoes. To keep the prayer hall clean, shoes are not allowed inside.

The mosque must have separate areas for men and women, so that they do not distract each other. It needs a marker, such as an alcove or niche in the wall, to indicate the direction for prayer (toward Mecca), and it must have a raised platform, called a *minbar*, for the imam to preach the Friday sermon.

The Importance of Pilgrimage

A pilgrim is someone who makes a special journey, called a pilgrimage, to a holy place. Places become centers of pilgrimage usually because they are associated with important people or events in the history of a religion. A pilgrimage is done as an act of worship. All major religions have their places of pilgrimage, but only Islam makes pilgrimage into a

Mosques are built in different styles in different countries. They often have domes and minarets. The dome amplifies the sound of the prayer-leader's voice so that everyone can hear what he says. The minaret is a tall tower from which the people are called to prayer by a man called a muezzin.

duty that its followers are expected to perform, if they are physically and financially able to do so.

The Hajj, the Great Pilgrimage to Mecca, is considered one of the Five Pillars of Islam. It takes place during the twelfth month of the year, called *Dhu-l-Hijjah*. Each year, some two million pilgrims gather in Mecca during the Hajj. Muslims spend the days of Hajj in regular prayer, reading the Qur'an, and performing the rituals of the pilgrimage. It is an opportunity for the pilgrims to renew their faith and to ask God to forgive their sins and transgressions.

Muslim pilgrims who participate in the Hajj are proud to walk in the footsteps of Muhammad, who himself made the pilgrimage. They also remember the earlier prophets Ibrahim (Abraham) and his son Isma'il (Ishmael). Mecca is such a holy city for Islam that only Muslims are allowed there, and they have to show their visas at checkpoints around the city.

The most important event of the Hajj takes place on the second day, on the Plain of Arafat, about 15 miles outside Mecca. Pilgrims must be there from noon to dusk. Most of them arrive in the morning, on foot or in buses and coaches. They encamp on the desert plain, creating a huge tent city. In the middle of this plain stands the Mount of Mercy, where pilgrims pray to God for

Educational Video

To view a documentary on the Hajj, scan here.

To accommodate the millions of pilgrims who come to Mecca from all over the world, a small city of tents is set up during the Hajj season at Mina, near Mecca.

forgiveness of their sins. The spectacle of many thousands of people swarming over this hill, their hands and faces raised to God in prayer, makes Muslims think of the Last Day—the day when, they believe, the world will end and God will judge each individual soul. Praying here at Hajj, on the Mount of Mercy, is intended to gain God's forgiveness and mercy, so that they will go to heaven when they die.

On the third day of Hajj, as the pilgrims travel back toward Mecca, they stop at the town of Mina. Here they

A visit to a high area outside of Mecca known as the Mount of Mercy is an important part of the Hajj ritual.

throw seven small pebbles at each of three stone pillars. This ritual, called "stoning the Devil," is an expression of their rejection of evil and their determination to withstand temptation.

Later, the pilgrims remove their special clothes, wash themselves, and cut their hair to show that they are no longer in *ihram*. They are now free to relax together and enjoy the festival of Eid al-Adha. The festival is held at

Mina and begins with a big feast. Pilgrims must offer an animal for sacrifice, if they can afford it. If they cannot, they will share in the third of the meat set aside for the poor. As there is too much meat to distribute all at once, the Saudi government has installed refrigeration.

The sacrifice of animals reminds Muslims of how Ibrahim was commanded by God to sacrifice his son Isma'il. At the last moment, God substituted a ram for the boy. Three times, the Devil is said to have tempted Ibrahim not to sacrifice his son, while also tempting Isma'il to run

During the Hajj, all pilgrims wear simple white robes. This is to symbolize that all Muslims are equal in the sight of Allah, regardless of their wealth or social status.

Pilgrims massed in the courtyard of the Great Mosque, walking around the Ka'bah. The Ka'bah, which takes its name from its cube shape, is an ancient shrine. It is covered in a black cloth embroidered with passages from the Qur'an.

away. But both father and son were determined to obey God, whatever the cost. It is said that together they drove away the Devil with stones, hence the traditional stoning of the three pillars at Mina.

Many pilgrims go on from Mecca to visit Medina, where Muhammad lived for the last ten years of his life, and is buried. Some also go on to Jerusalem, the third holy city in Islam.

The Sacred Ka'bah

Muslims spend their lives praying in the direction of the *Ka'bah* before they ever get the chance to see it—if ever they do. The Ka'bah is an ancient building in the center of the Great Mosque in Mecca, and the pilgrimage starts with the pilgrims circling it seven times continuously in an anti-clockwise direction. Muslims believe that it was the first house of prayer on earth, built by Adam, the first man, as a replica of the house of prayer in heaven. Later, the prophet Ibrahim is said to have rebuilt the Ka'bah with the help of his son Isma'il.

In one corner is the Black Stone, which pilgrims try to touch or kiss during the Hajj. This stone was part of the Ka'bah long before the time of Muhammad. There is a story of how once, when the Ka'bah was being repaired, Muhammad was asked to mediate between the chieftains of Mecca, who each wanted the honor of replacing the stone in its wall. Muhammad suggested that each chief should hold a corner of a cloak on which the stone was carried, and Muhammad himself lifted the stone into place.

A pilgrim prepares to drink water that was drawn from the Zamzam Well, a spring near the Ka'bah that Muslims believe provided water for Abraham's son Ishmael to drink.

During Muhammad's time, the Ka'bah housed many religious idols. When Muhammad and his Muslim army conquered Mecca in 629 CE, he destroyed the idols in the Ka'bah. Today, the building remains completely empty as a sign to Muslims that they must never try to make images of God.

 ## Text-Dependent Questions

1. What is *wudu*?
2. Why does a Muslim kneel on the floor with their forehead touching the ground when praying?
3. During what month of the Islamic calendar does the Hajj take place?

 ## Research Project

Using the Internet or your school library, do some research to answer the question "Do religious believers need a special place of worship?"

Those who agree will say that believers should be allowed to give God their very best, whatever it costs. The design of the building can create a setting that helps people to worship. Those who disagree with this perspective believe that it is not right to spend money on places of worship when people are starving all over the world. Moreover, they contend, if God is everywhere, what need is there for special places of worship?

Present your conclusion in a two-page report, providing examples from your research that support your answer.

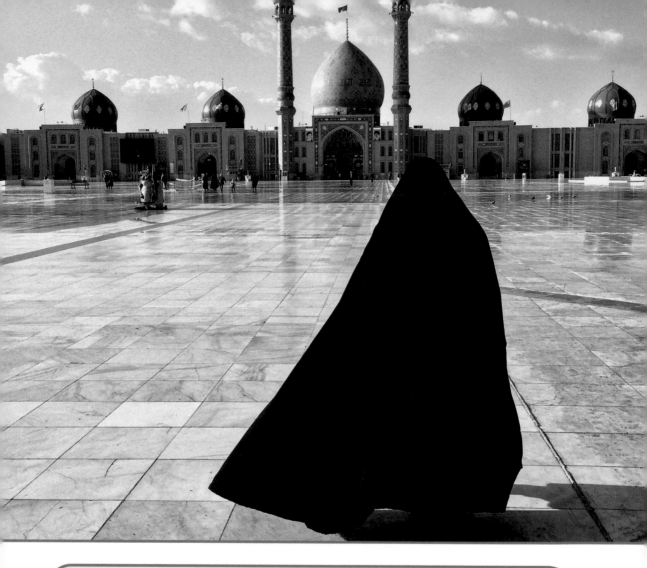

 ## Words to Understand in This Chapter

haram—anything unlawful or not permitted in Islam.

hijab—"veil," most often used to describe the headscarf or modest dress Muslims believe should be worn by women.

jihad—personal, individual struggle against evil in the way of Allah; also, defense of the Muslim community, a "holy war."

Shari'ah—Islamic law based on the Qur'an and the Sunnah (a collection of model practices).

Sunnah—model practices, customs, and traditions of the Prophet Muhammad.

In some strict Muslim countries, such as Iran, women are required to wear a long outer garment called a **chador** *over their other clothes when they appear in public.*

5 Muslim Values in the Modern World

Muslims claim that their values have not changed since the time of Muhammad and the revelation of the Qur'an. They are based on truthfulness and honest living; responsibility and trustworthiness; kindness and compassion; forgiveness and generosity; humility and modesty; fortitude and courage.

The most important authority in life for Muslims is Allah, whose words, they believe, are recorded in the Qur'an. What God tells Muslims to do there, they should do; and what God forbids, they should not do. Muslims also look to the life of the Prophet Muhammad for guidance. Muhammad's practice, or way of doing things, is called the *Sunnah*. In his Farewell Speech, Muhammad said, "I leave behind me two things, the Qur'an, and my example, the

Sunnah, and if you follow these you will never go astray." Islamic Law is called the Shar'iah, the "straight path," and is based on the Qur'an and the Sunnah. The Hadith, stories about Muhammad and his companions in the early Muslim community, are also referred to as a guide for the faithful.

Islam requires certain behaviors, such as the Five Pillars, to be observed by all Muslims. The religion also absolutely forbids certain practices—for example, the worship of gods other than Allah, or engaging in adultery or theft, are completely forbidden. The Qur'an and Sunnah list many actions that that are approved and others that are not. However, the world has changed greatly since Muhammad received his revelations in the seventh century, and today Muslims must determine for themselves how certain actions should be treated. Many modern issues, including organ transplantation and the use of technology, come into this last category. Often, these decisions are left to the individual's conscience.

Marriage and Family Life

Marriage and family life are at the heart of Muslim society. Marriage is seen as the best channel for sexual desires, to allow Muslims expression in having children and grandchildren in a secure setting, and to give people companionship with a partner.

Because of the importance of marriage, in many traditional Muslim countries it was the custom for parents to arrange their childrens' marriages. Marriage is seen as joining two families together, rather than just two individuals.

A Muslim couple getting married in Malaysia. They were introduced to each other by their parents, rather than having met each other by chance. Although arranged marriages are very unusual among American Muslims, the practice remains common in most Muslim countries, where Western-style dating and socializing are often not permitted.

A boy's parents will look for a suitable partner for their son, and approach the girl's parents. The boy and girl meet in a family gathering, and both should give their consent. An arranged marriage should not be a forced marriage, however, as this is against Islamic law. In the West, most people marry someone whom they love. In an arranged marriage, it is believed that love will grow in time between the couple.

Strictly speaking, polygamy—the practice of a man having more than one wife at a time—is permitted in Islam, although it is not common. This practice goes back to Muhammad's time, when many young men were killed in battle, leaving widows and children in need of support and protection. After his first wife, Kadijah, died, Muhammad married at least nine more wives. The Qur'an states that a man may take up to four wives at a time, provided that he treats all of them equally.

Some wealthy Muslims still follow this practice in countries where it is permitted. However, for the most part polygamy is considered unusual, and not recommended, by many Muslims today. Some Muslim countries have outlawed the practice.

Adultery—having sexual relations with someone other than your husband or wife—is a very grave sin in Islam and is strictly forbidden. Muslims believe that the people involved have acted irresponsibly, giving way to lust and showing no concern for other adults and any children who may be affected by their actions. Adultery threatens a marriage and family life, besides increasing the risk of illegiti-

A happy Muslim family. Although Islamic law permits Muslim men to have more than one wife, the practice of polygamy is extremely rare. It is expensive to keep more than one wife, and many countries have laws that forbid polygamy.

mate children. In countries where *Shari'ah* is the law of the land, punishment for adultery can be very severe.

Islam does recognize that a marriage may not work out, and does not condemn a married couple to a life of misery by refusing to consider the possibility that it can be better for a couple to separate and lead new lives. Muslims would prefer to avoid divorce, but it is permitted when it is not possible to save the relationship. It is far better for a Muslim to divorce and remarry than to commit adultery, which is forbidden. Married couples are separated openly and legally with their rights protected.

Women's Rights in Islam

Islam teaches that men and women are equal before God, but that he has made them different so that they can handle different roles and responsibilities in life. Muslims believe that motherhood is a blessing from God and an important part of being a woman, and that a woman's first duty is to

Women in some tolerant Asian countries, such as Indonesia and Malaysia, often enjoy greater freedoms and career choices than Muslim women in other countries.

her family. Women are not thought of as being less important than men. Their influence in bringing up their children is of utmost importance, and mothers are given great respect.

Many Muslim women are highly educated and have responsible jobs, such as teaching or being a doctor. Some have achieved important public positions, such as Benazir Bhutto of Pakistan, who in 1988 became the first woman to lead a Muslim state, or Ameenah Gurib, who was elected president of Mauritius in 2015. But most Muslim women in a profession would expect to take a break from their careers to look after their children when they are young.

The cultural traditions of some Muslim countries, such as Egypt, Morocco, and Saudi Arabia, prevent women from doing much outside the home. Saudi Arabia is particularly strict, as women are not allowed to go out in public without being fully veiled, and many women cannot work or drive a car. In other Muslim countries, such as Turkey and Indonesia, both girls and boys are educated and may go on to study at a university and have a professional career. In the West, most Muslim girls tend to have similar career plans to their non-Muslim friends.

All Muslims—men and women—are taught to dress modestly. This is required in the Qur'an. However, modest dress is interpreted differently in different Muslim countries. In public, Muslim women are generally expected to wear the *hijab*, a scarf that covers their hair. In some conservative countries, such as Saudi Arabia, Iran, and Afghanistan, women are expected to wear the *chador* or the *burqa*. These are garments that covers the woman from head to toe. When wearing the *burqa*, even the woman's face is covered by a mesh veil.

Many Muslim women say they feel comfortable with the Islamic dress code. They believe it protects them from unwanted attention from men, and helps them to be treated equally and with respect.

Respect for the Elderly and Children

Muslims have traditionally lived in extended families. A new bride will move to her husband's home and live there with his parents and other relatives. In this type of family, people of all ages have to learn to get on together and everyone is looked after, from the little children to the great-grandparents.

There is much love for children in Islam, and couples often have large families. Children, in turn, are brought up to respect their elders and to accept the fact that the younger generations will be responsible for looking after the elders as they grow old and frail.

The Qur'an requires Muslims to treat their elders with respect. Qur'an 17: 23–24 says, "Your Lord has commanded you … to be kind to your parents. If one or both of them

Educational Video

Scan for a short clip of Shiites celebrating Ashura.

reach old age when they are with you, do not speak impatiently to them or scold them, but speak to them respectfully. Act humbly toward them and show kindness and say, "My Lord, show them mercy, as they cared for me when I was a child."

Prohibited Vices

The Qur'an forbids Muslims from drinking alcohol, such as beer, wine, and spirits. In many western societies, drinking alcohol is associated with special events such as restaurant meals, parties, and weddings, but it is also an integral part

North Africa and the Middle East are the historical heartlands of the Islamic faith. Many of the most important Muslim shrines are found in Saudi Arabia.

Devout Muslims are not permitted to drink alcohol, use recreational drugs, or participate in gambling. The Qur'an says that these things are **haram**.

of everyday social relations for many people. Unfortunately it is also associated with uncontrolled behavior and with road accidents in which innocent people are killed or injured by drunken drivers. Excessive drinking can also cause fatal medical conditions such as cirrhosis of the liver. Some people become addicted to alcohol, and it is difficult for alcoholics to give up drinking in societies where alcohol is easily obtained.

There was similar abuse of alcohol in the Arab societies of Muhammad's day. The Prophet believed that the harm that alcohol caused far outweighed the pleasure that it brought. Islam teaches that people should respect and look after the bodies Allah has given them. Also, it is important that Muslims are in full possession of their senses when they pray—which they do five times a day, four of these after midday, when people are most inclined to have an alcoholic drink.

Islam permits the use of medicinal drugs, but drug use for recreation is forbidden, for the same reason that drinking alcohol is not allowed. Drugs can affect people's judgement and damage their health. There are social reasons too. Drug addicts can find it hard to hold down a job, and some commit crimes to feed their habit. Smoking tobacco is not forbidden to Muslims, however. This might be because the dangers of nicotine were not recognized at the time the Qur'an was written.

Islam forbids all forms of gambling, which in Arabic is called *maisir*. The Qur'an teaches that people should earn money for themselves and their family through honest work, not through games of chance.

The Sanctity of Life, and Modern Medical Developments

Islam teaches that all life is sacred because it is given by God, the Creator. This belief is at the heart of all Muslim teaching on mercy-killing, suicide, abortion, contraception, execution, war, and murder.

Muslims believe that each person's lifetime is supremely important because it is that person's chance to prepare for the life to come. The length of one's life on Earth should be left to God to decide, and it is wrong for anyone to cut short a life except through due process of law. The Qur'an states, "No one dies unless Allah permits. The term of every life is fixed."

From this Islamic principle, suicide and murder are clearly wrong. Nor is euthanasia permitted. This is sometimes called mercy-killing—helping people to die quickly and avoid more pain when their suffering is beyond medical help.

Abortion—terminating a pregnancy—is also forbidden, unless the mother's life is at risk. A pregnancy can terminate naturally, but it can also be brought on medically. Modern technology can produce photographs of a fetus developing in the womb, so one can no longer think of a fetus as a "blob of jelly" that becomes a person only at birth. Islam teaches that the soul enters the fetus at 120 days (four months) after conception, and if a miscarriage takes place after this time, or the baby is stillborn, then it would be buried in the same way as any other Muslim.

Birth control is allowed in Islam if it prevents conception taking place. Therefore, using a condom is permitted, but using the morning-after pill is not, because the child may already have been conceived, and this would cause an abortion. Natural methods of contraception, such as withdrawal, were practiced in Muhammad's time, and he permitted it. Muslims believe that creation ultimately lies in Allah's hands, so they should not prevent a birth if He wills it.

Modern medical techniques, such as embryo technology, organ transplants, and the separation of conjoined twins, have raised issues for Islam that are obviously not dealt with directly in the Qur'an. In such cases, the basic Qur'anic principles have to be applied to the new situations.

For instance, artificial insemination by the husband, or in vitro fertilization of the wife's egg by the husband's sperm, is usually acceptable because these methods are helping the normal process for that couple to have their baby. But artificial insemination by a donor, and not the husband, is not acceptable because this is seen as similar to the sin of adultery, or having sex with someone other than one's husband or wife.

Doctors can now often separate twins that are joined at birth. This may mean that one of the twins will die, for instance if they share a heart. Then, the operation would only be performed if both twins were likely to die without it. Even so, it is difficult for Muslim parents to give consent to such an operation, knowing that saving the life of one of their children will hasten the death of another. The decision may be taken out of the parents' hands, and the babies are made wards of court, so that a judge decides on the best course of action.

Muslims have generally been opposed to organ transplants because of their belief in the resurrection, or rising up, of the body after death, at the Last Day. This is also the reason why they bury their dead, rather than cremate them. They think it wrong to tamper with the body that God has created. However, this has caused problems for Muslims suffering from liver disease, which is particularly prevalent in the Asian population, and some Muslim organizations now permit Muslims to donate and receive organs.

Islamic Dietary Restrictions

Although the life of an animal is also sacred to Muslims, they believe it is permissible to kill animals for food, but not

In Western countries like the United States and United Kingdom, Muslims must purchase meat from shops that prepare their products according to the halal *guidelines.*

to waste an animal's life. Muhammad lived in Arabia, a region with large expanses of desert. People kept herds of goats and sheep for food, because it was so dificult to grow food by farming the dry land. Without more water, crops such as vegetables could not be grown. The main agricultural crop came from date palms, which grow in desert oases.

There are strict food laws in Islam, just as there are in Judaism and Hinduism. Food that is "permitted" is called *halal* and that which is not permitted is called *haram*. All fish, fruits, and vegetables, and all grains, are permitted. Meat is permitted as long as it is slaughtered correctly—except for meet from a pig, because Muslims consider pigs to be "unclean" animals.

The *halal* method of slaughter is to slit the animal's throat with a very sharp knife, so that the animal does not feel the cut and quickly loses consciousness as the blood pours out. This is believed to be the most merciful method of killing. The name of God is pronounced over the animal in a prayer to remind Muslims that they are taking a life that comes from God—for all life is sacred.

War and *Jihad*

Because Muslims believe in the sanctity of life, they are opposed to unlawful killing. However, the taking of life by lawful execution or when war has been declared, is considered to be justified.

Most people dislike the idea of war. However, in desperate situations, parents may feel proud of their children who

Muslims demonstrate against Israel's treatment of Palestinian Arabs. Most Muslims around the world feel that Israel has illegally taken the Palestinians' land.

are going off to war, while still worrying about their safety. In the same way, some religions have drawn up rules that make war permissible—a justified "holy war." In Islam, a war is considered to be holy if it is "in the cause of Allah"—waged for justice and the right to practice Islam, and not for personal gain. In Islam, holy war is called *jihad*.

According to Muslims, a holy war should only be undertaken as a last resort. It must have the authority of Muslim religious leaders and produce the minimum suffering necessary to win. Violence should stop when the enemy has surrendered. The Qur'an also says that women, children, the elderly, and the disabled should not be harmed by the *jihad*.

The Prophet Muhammad described two types of jihad. The "Greater Jihad" is the struggle within each person to resist evil and submit to Allah's plan for their life. The "Lesser Jihad" involves taking up weapons to fight.

Muslims are taught that they should fight against wrongdoing and oppression, and not just allow these things to carry on. They should be prepared to give up everything, even their own lives, for the cause of right. In this sense, all Muslims should be fighters—but this does not necessarily mean they have to be aggressive or take up weapons. Someone can struggle against evil in society, for example, through political channels. They can speak out against injustice and make their views heard.

Islamic Fundamentalism

In the fifteenth and sixteenth centuries, the Muslim civilization began to wane. During this time, European countries began to explore and conquer territories all over the globe, including Muslim lands in Africa, Asia, and the Middle East. During the colonial period, Muslims in these regions were encouraged to adopt Western-style governments and legal codes, as well as other elements of European societies such as modern industries, clothing, and culture. As the effort to break up colonial empires grew in the twentieth century, some Muslim leaders began to encourage Muslims to reclaim their religious and cultural heritage. Those who wanted to once again make Islam the center of both religious and political life became known as Islamic fundamentalists. Today, the term *Islamist* is used to refer to people with this worldview.

Two early Islamist groups that were very influential were the Muslim Brotherhood, established in Egypt in 1928 by Hasan al-Banna, and the Islamic Society, founded by Mawlana Abu al-Ala Mawdudi in India in 1941. These groups wanted to return Islam to an earlier, purer form, and criticized those who wanted to establish Western-style governments in Muslim lands. Both al-Banna and Mawdudi claimed that Islam and the Qur'an offered everything Muslims needed—they did not need to turn to the West for ideas about how to govern themselves or run their societies.

The European colonial system, in which countries exploited the natural resources and people of the lands that they ruled, lasted until the end of World War II in 1945. Many of today's nations became independent during the 1940s, 1950s, and 1960s. At first, many of the governments were secular Western-style regimes. But over time Islamist groups became more powerful. In 1979, Iranian Islamists inspired by a Shiite religious leader named Ayatollah Khomeini overthrew the US-supported government of the Shah. Khomeini soon established a government run by religious authorities, with Shari'ah as the law of the land. Subsequent rulers of Iran have acted as both religious and political leaders.

The success of the Iranian revolution inspired Muslims around the world to reassert their faith and place an increased emphasis on personal and community religious

In late 2010 and early 2011, anti-government protests began to occur in a number of Arab countries, beginning with the North African country of Tunisia. The protests—which became known as the "Arab Spring"—soon spread to Egypt, Bahrain, Libya, Saudi Arabia, Jordan, Yemen, and many other countries in the Middle East. They were aimed at improving the political circumstances and living conditions of Arab Muslims. In Egypt, the longtime president was overthrown and an Islamist government came to power. However, that government was soon replaced in a military coup.

life. Islamic political organizations became an even more important part of the political process in Muslim countries during the 1980s and 1990s. Islamists successfully participated in elections in Turkey, Malaysia, Indonesia, and other countries. Though their concerns remained mostly domestic, Islamists made themselves heard on international issues as well, such the conflict between Israelis and Palestinian Arabs, the invasion of Afghanistan by the Soviet Union, United Nations sanctions against Iraq following the Persian Gulf War, and repressive efforts against Muslims in Bosnia, Chechnya, and Kashmir during the 1990s.

Islam and Terrorism

During the 1980s and 1990s, small militant Islamist groups also began to grow and spread. They demanded total obedience to Allah in every aspect of life, and asserted their religious duty to commit *jihad* against their oppressors. To defend their cause, these groups were willing to take up arms and resist their opponents in their own countries and elsewhere. Among them are Hezbollah ("party of God"), a Shiite political force in Lebanon; Hamas, which promotes Palestinian nationalism; and Islamic Jihad, a Palestinian group with close ties to Iran. The most notorious group to Americans was al-Qaeda, which carried out many terrorist strikes against US targets, including the September 11, 2001, attacks against the World Trade Center and Pentagon, which killed nearly 3,000 people.

Though they comprise only a small minority of

Islamists, the threat that violent groups pose to military forces and everyday citizens have unfortunately led many in the West to adopt the stereotype of all Islamist activists—and sometimes even all Muslims—as violent. This is not really fair, as millions of Muslims reject terrorism and the killing of innocents. All people must be careful not to judge any religion by the actions of a few people who claim to be believers in that faith.

 Text-Dependent Questions

1. What is polygamy? Is it permitted in Islam?
2. What female Muslim was elected president of Mauritius in 2015?
3. What is the difference between *halal* and *haram*?

 Research Project

Using the Internet or your school library, do some research to answer the question, "Is violence ever justified? On one hand, some people argue that the principle of "an eye for an eye" would leave the whole world blind. If people are strong enough, they contend, they can overcome evil with love. Others believe that while violence is wrong, it may also be the lesser of two evils—for example, it is good to overthrow a dictator whose actions cause innocent people to suffer. Present your conclusion in a two-page report, providing examples from your research that support your answer.

Religious Demographics

U.S. & Canada about 5.6 million people

Canada about 25 million people

U.S. about 225 million people

U.S. about 0.575 million

North and South America about 10 million people

Latin America about 543 million people

Europe about 2.1 million people

Europe about 0.5 million people

Europe about 550 million people

Europe about 50 million people

Israel about 5.6 million people

Africa about 518 million people

Africa about 475 million people

Asia about 1179 million people

Asia about 350 million people

Asia about 550 million people

India about 18 million people

Asia about 950 million people

Australia and Oceania about 24 million people

Australia and Oceania about 0.7 million people

Christians
about 2.2 billion people

Muslims
about 1.6 billion people

Sikh
about 23 million people

Hindus
about 1 billion people

Jews
about 14 million people

Buddhist
about 576 million people

| **Christian** 31.5% | **Islam** 22.3% | **No religion** 15.4% | **Hindu** 14.0% | **Buddhist** 5.3% | **Sikhism** 0.3% | **Judaism** 0.2% | **Others** 11% |

Hinduism

Founded
Developed gradually in prehistoric times

Number of followers
Around 1 billion

Holy Places
River Ganges, especially at Varanasi
(Benares). Several other places in India

Holy Books
Vedas, Upanishads,
Mahabharata, Rarnayana

Holy Symbol
Aum

Buddhism

Founded
535 BCE in Northern India

Number of followers
Around 576 million

Holy Places
Bodh Gaya, Sarnath, both in northern India

Holy Books
Tripitaka

Holy Symbol
Eight-spoked wheel

Sikhism

Founded
Northwest India, 15th century CE

Number of followers
Around 23 million

Holy Places
There are five important, takhts, or seats of
high authority: in Amritsar, Patna Sahib,
Anandpur Sahib, Nanded, and Talwandi

Holy Books
The Guru Granth Sahib

Holy Symbol
The Khanda, the symbol
of the Khalsa

Christianity

Founded
Around 30 CE, Jerusalem

Number of followers
Around 2.2 billion

Holy Places
Jerusalem and other sites
associated with the life of Jesus

Holy Books
The Bible
(Old and New Testament)

Holy Symbol
Cross

Judaism

Founded
In what is now Israel, around 2,000 BCE

Number of followers
Around 14 million

Holy Places
Jerusalem, especially
the Western Wall

Holy Books
The Torah

Holy Symbol
Seven-branched menorah (candle stand)

Islam

Founded
610 CE on the Arabian Peninsula

Number of followers
Around 1.6 billion

Holy Places
Makkah and Madinah, in Saudi Arabia

Holy Books
The Qur'an

Holy Symbol
Crescent and star

Quick Reference: Islam

Worldwide distribution

There are roughly 1.6 billion Muslims in the world. This means more than one in five people is a Muslim. Islam is the world's fastest-growing religion. Muslims live on all populated continents of the world, although most live in Asia, Africa, and the Middle East. Islam is the third-largest religion in the United States, after Christianity and Judaism.

Islam, as we know it, began on the Arabian Peninsula during the time of Muhammad, but quickly spread beyond Arabia. Only 20 percent of Muslims today are Arabs. Mecca, in Saudi Arabia, remains the religious center of Islam.

The countries with the highest number of Muslims are Indonesia with 210 million, and Pakistan with 170 million. Both are densely populated.

Language

Arabic is the language of the Muslim holy book, the Qur'an, because Muhammad lived in Arabia (now Saudi Arabia). Arabic is also the dominant spoken language in the Muslim countries of Jordan, Iraq, and Syria and also the countries of North Africa, down to Mauritania in western Africa, and including the Sudan, which is south of Egypt.

Festivals

The dates of Muslim festivals are set in the Islamic (lunar) calendar and do not change. However, because this calendar is 10 or 11 days shorter than the 365-day solar year, the festivals occur on different days of the Western calendar each year. Important festivals to Muslims include the first day of Muharram (New Year's day), Ashura, (9–10 Muharram), Maulid ul Nabi (12 Rabia Awwal), Lailat-ul-Isra'wal Miraj (27 Rajab), Lailat-ul-Barat (14–15 Shaban), the sacred month of Ramadan, Lailat-ul-Qadr (27 Ramadan), Eid al-Fitr (1 Shawwal), and Eid al-Adha (10–13 Dhu al-Hijja).

Above: Muslims participate in butchering a cow for Eid al-Adha, the feast of sacrifice that is celebrated each year.

Opposite: an imam leads Muslims in their Friday prayers.

Islam Timeline

570	Birth of Muhammad.
610	Muhammad receives the first revelations from Allah, which will later be recorded in the Qur'an.
613	Muhammad begins preaching publicly.
622	Muhammad and his followers begin the hijrah, or migration, from Mecca to Medina, an event that marks the beginning of the Muslim era.
630	An Arab Muslim army led by Muhammad takes control of Mecca.
632	Muhammad dies, and the era of the "rightly guided caliphs" begins when Abu Bakr is chosen as the first caliph.
656	Ali becomes the fourth caliph, sparking a civil war in the Muslim community.
661	Ali is assassinated, and Muawiyya declares himself caliph. The political center of Islam moves to Damascus in Syria.
680	Ali's son Hussein is killed, with his family and many supporters, at the Battle of Karbala.
683	The Umayyad succession of caliphs begins. Based in Syria, their rule extends eastward to the borders of India and China and westward to Spain.

749	The Abbasids overthrow the Umayyads.
820	al-Shafii, who created an authoritative methodology for developing Sharia, dies.
874	The power of the Abbasid caliphs begins to wane; local dynasties start to establish rule throughout the Abbasid empire.
1058	The jurist and mystic al-Ghazali is born; he eventually helps make Sufism accepted in Islam.
1099	The European Crusaders capture Jerusalem and establish four Crusader kingdoms.
1187	Muslim forces under Saladin defeat the Crusaders and recapture Jerusalem.
1453	The armies of the Ottoman Turks capture Constantinople, bringing the thousand-year rule of the Byzantine empire to an end.
1502	The Safavid Empire is established in Iran; Shia Islam becomes the state religion.
1526	The Moghul Empire is founded in India.
1765	Great Britain forces the Moghul emperor to give up control of part of India; the British will eventually control all of the area of modern-day India and Pakistan.
1919	In the conference that ends World War I, the Arab lands of the defeated Ottoman empire are divided into small states and placed under the control of France or Great Britain.
1923	Turkey establishes the first secular government in a Muslim country.

1928	Hasan al-Banna founds the Muslim Brotherhood in Egypt.
1941	Mawlana Abu al-Ala Mawdudi establishes the Islamic Society in India.
1947	Pakistan is created as an Islamic state.
1948	Israel is founded, and immediately fights a two-year war for independence.
1967	Israel defeats the combined forces of Egypt, Jordan, and Syria in the Six-Day War.
1978	U.S. President Jimmy Carter helps to negotiate a peace treaty between Israel and Egypt.
1979	Revolution grips Iran and the Islamic Republic comes to power.
1980	Iraq invades Iran, setting off an eight-year conflict in the Persian Gulf.
1991	An international coalition of nations, led by the United States, attacks Iraq, forcing it to withdraw from Kuwait, which it had invaded and annexed in 1990.
1995	During ethnic fighting in Bosnia, Serbian troops overrun a U.N. "safe area" at Srebrenica; an estimated 7,000 Muslim men and boys are massacred.
2000	The Israeli-Palestinian peace process fails, and the second intifada begins.
2001	On September 11, terrorists crash hijacked airplanes into the World Trade Center in

New York and the Pentagon near Washington, D.C.; the U.S. responds by attacking Afghanistan and overthrowing the Taliban regime, which had sheltered the al-Qaeda terrorist network. This action is condemned by many Muslims.

2005 The Fiqh Council of North America issues a *fatwa* condemning terrorism and extremism.

2007 In January, Keith Ellison is sworn in to the U.S. House of Representatives, becoming the first Muslim member of Congress.

2012 Mohamed Morsi, a member of the Muslim Brotherhood, is sworn in as president after he wins Egypt's first competitive presidential election. Morsi would be ousted in June of the following year by a military coup.

2013 Islamist groups fighting in Iraq and Syria form the Islamic State of Iraq and the Levant (ISIL), which is able to capture and hold territory in both countries.

2014 In June, the Islamic State of Iraq and the Levant declares a caliphate in the territory they control, stretching from Aleppo in northwestern Syria to the eastern Iraqi province of Diyala.

2016 Islamic extremist Ahmad Khan Rahami is arrested for bombings in New York and New Jersey.

Series Glossary of Key Terms

afterlife—a term that refers to a continuation of existence beyond the natural world, or after death.

BCE and CE—alternatives to the traditional Western designation of calendar eras, which used the birth of Jesus as a dividing line. BCE stands for "Before the Common Era," and is equivalent to BC ("Before Christ"). Dates labeled CE, or "Common Era," are equivalent to *Anno Domini* (AD, or "the Year of Our Lord").

chant—the rhythmic speaking or singing of words or sounds, intended to convey emotion in worship or to express the chanter's spiritual side. Chants can be conducted either on a single pitch or with a simple melody involving a limited set of notes, and often include a great deal of repetition.

creation—the beginnings of humanity, earth, life, and the universe. According to most religions, creation was a deliberate act by a supreme being.

deity (or god)—a supernatural being, usually considered to have significant power. Deities/gods are worshipped and considered sacred by human beings. Some deities are believed to control time and fate, to be the ultimate judges of human worth and behavior, and to be the designers and creators of the Earth or the universe. Others are believed to control natural phenomena, such as lightning, floods, and storms. They can assume a variety of forms, but are frequently depicted as having human or animal form, as well as specific personalities and characteristics.

hymn—a song specifically written as a song of praise, adoration or prayer, typically addressed to a god or deity.

miracle—according to many religions, a miracle is an unusual example of divine intervention in the universe by a god or deity, often one in which natural laws are overruled, suspended, or modified.

prayer—an effort to communicate with a deity or god, or another form of spiritual entity. Prayers are usually intended to offer praise, to make a request, or simply to express the person's thoughts and emotions.

prophecy—the prediction of future events, thanks to either direct or indirect communication with a deity or god. The term prophecy is also used to describe the revelation of divine will.

religion—a system of belief concerning the supernatural, sacred, or divine; and the moral codes, practices, values, institutions and rituals associated with such belief. There are many different religions in the world today.

ritual—a formal, predetermined set of symbolic actions generally performed in a particular environment at a regular, recurring interval. The actions that make up a ritual often include, but are not limited to, such things as recitation, singing, group processions, repetitive dance, and manipulation of sacred objects. The general purpose of rituals is to engage a group of people in unified worship, in order to strengthen their communal bonds.

saint—a term that refers to someone who is considered to be exceptionally virtuous and holy. It can be applied to both the living and the dead and is an acceptable term in most of the world's popular religions. A saint is held up as an example of how all other members of the religious community should act.

worship—refers to specific acts of religious praise, honor, or devotion, typically directed to a supernatural being such as a deity or god. Typical acts of worship include prayer, sacrifice, rituals, meditation, holidays and festivals, pilgrimages, hymns or psalms, the construction of temples or shrines, and the creation of idols that represent the deity.

Organizations to Contact

Muslim Association of America
733 15th St NW, Suite 1102
Washington D.C. 20005

Islamic Society of North America
(ISNA)
6555 South County Road (750 East)
P.O. Box 38
Plainfield, IN 46168
Phone: 317.839.8157
Website: www.isna.net

American League of Muslims
P.O. Box 2330
Brockton, MA

Islamic Assembly of North America
3588 Plymouth Road, Suite 270
Ann Arbor, MI 48105

National Islamic Association
239 Roseville Avenue
Newark, NJ 07107

The Canadian Society of Muslims
P.O. Box 143 Station P
Toronto, ON M5S 2SP

Further Reading

Armstrong, Karen. *Muhammad: A Prophet for Our Time*. New York: HarperCollins, 2007.

Aslan, Reza. *No god but God: The Origins, Evolution, and Future of Islam*. New York: Random House, 2011.

Bowker, John. *World Religions: The Great Faiths Explored and Explained*. London: Dorling Kindersley Ltd., 2006.

Harris, Sam, and Maajid Nawaz. *Islam and the Future of Tolerance: A Dialogue*. Cambridge, Mass.: Harvard University Press, 2015.

Mansfield, Peter. *A History of the Middle East*. 4th ed. revised and updated by Nicholas Pelham. New York: Penguin Books, 2013.

McDermott, Gerald R. *World Religions: An Indispensable Introduction*. Nashville, Tenn.: Thomas Nelson, 2011.

Prothero, Stephen. *God Is Not One: The Eight Rival Religions that Run the World*. New York: HarperCollins, 2010.

Smith, Huston. *The World's Religions*. New York: HarperCollins, 2009.

Internet Resources

http://islam.com
A portal with information about Islam, including discussion forums, articles, and links to other resources.

http://islam.uga.edu
A comprehensive collection of essays and links to online sources on Islamic history, culture, sects, law, and contemporary issues, collected by Dr. Alan Godlas, a professor at the University of Georgia.

http://www.fordham.edu/halsall/islam/islamsbook.html
Fordham University provides this online Islamic History Sourcebook, with links to texts from every period in the history of Islam, as well as maps and other resources.

http://america.aljazeera.com
The English-language website of the Arabic news service Al Jazeera provides articles and videos on breaking news, as well as feature stories that provide background material, including profiles of leaders and essays reacting to major events.

http://www.cair.com/
The Council on American-Islamic Relations (CAIR) is an organization dedicated to providing an Islamic perspective on issues of importance to the American people.

http://www.pbs.org/wgbh/pages/frontline/shows/muslims
A special installment of the PBS program *Frontline* that examines contemporary Islam through profiles of and interviews with Muslims in the United States, Africa, the Middle East, and Asia.

http://www.pewresearch.org/topics/muslims-and-islam
This page run by the Pew Research Center provides links to polls and articles about the opinions and attitudes of people living in the Muslim World.

https://www.cia.gov/library/publications/the-world-factbook
The CIA World Factbook is a convenient source of basic information about any country in the world. This site includes links to a page on each country with religious, geographic, demographic, economic, and governmental data.

http://daralislam.org
The website of Dar al Islam, a non-profit organization that promotes understanding between Muslims and non-Muslims in the United States. Includes recent news and academic articles on Islamic politics, culture, and history.

Publisher's Note: The websites listed on these pages were active at the time of publication. The publisher is not responsible for websites that have changed their address or discontinued operation since the date of publication. The publisher reviews and updates the websites each time the book is reprinted.

Index

Abbasid dynasty, 36–38
abortion, 82
Abraham. *See* Ibrahim (Abraham)
Abu Bakr, 27–28
Adam, 21, 23, 67
adultery, 74–75
Aisha (daughter of Abu Bakr),
    30–31
al-Qaeda, 90
alcohol, 79–81
Ali (Ali ibn Abi Talib), 8, 17–18,
    24, *25*
    as successor to Muhammad, 28,
        30–31, *32*, 33
Ali (son of Hussein), 34
Allah, 8, 9, 10–11, 15, 21, 27, 42
    images of, 11
    names for, 12
    See also Islam
angels, 10, 22
aqiqah ceremony, 45–46, *47*
Ashura, 54, 96

birth control, 82

calendar, Islamic, 40, 47–49, 52–53,
    54–55, 62, 96
chador, *71*, 77–78
charity. *See* zakah (charity)
Christianity, 15, 22, 23, 29–30, 37,
    92, 94, 95

circumcision, 45–46
clothing, *71*, 77–78
coming-of-age rituals, 41
    See also rituals
Crusades, 37

demographics, religion, 92–94
dietary restrictions, 84–85
drugs, *80*, 81
Druze (sect), 19

Egypt, 15, 29, 34, 77, 88, *89*
Eid al-Adha, 50, 52, 64–65, 96
Eid al-Fitr, 50–52, 96
euthanasia, 81, 82

family. *See* marriage and family life
fasting (sawm), 40, 42–43, *44*,
    51–52, *53*
Fatima (daughter of Muhammad),
    28
festivals, Islamic, 40, 42, 43, *44*,
    49–55, 64–65, 96
Five Pillars of Islam, 41–45, 57, 62,
    72
    See also Islam
fundamentalism, Islamic, 87–90

gambling, *80*, 81

Hadith, 20, 27, 72

Numbers in ***bold italics*** refer to captions.

Hajj (pilgrimage), 40, 42, 50, 52, 56, 62–67, 69
halal guidelines, 40, 52, *84*
Hamas, 90
haram practices, 70, 79–81, 85
Hassan (son of Ali), 33
Hezbollah, 90
hijab, 70, 77
Hijrah, 40, 49–50
Hussein (son of Ali), 33–34, 54

Ibadiyyah (sect), 19
Ibrahim (Abraham), 15, 23, 62, 65, 67, *68*
idols, 21, 22, 24, 27, 69
India, 13, 34, 36, 37, 88
Indonesia, 13, *14, 76*, 77, 90
Iran, *14*, 18, 34, 37, *71*, 77, 88
Iraq, 18, 37, 38, 90
Isa (Jesus), 23, 27
Islam, 9–12, 15
    calendar of, 40, 47–49, 52–53, 54–55, 62, 96
    and dietary restrictions, 84–85
    and the elderly and children, 78–79
    festivals in, 40, 42, 43, *44*, 49–55, 64–65, 96
    Five Pillars of, 41–45, 57, 62, 72
    and fundamentalism, 87–90
    history of, 9, 13, 21–24, 27–39, 95
    and marriage and family life, 72–76, 77, 78–79
    number of followers of, 9, 13, *14*, 15, 92, 94, 95
    and prohibited vices, 79–81
    quick reference to, 95–96
    rituals of, 41, 45–47
    and the sanctity of life, 81–83, 85
    sects of, 8, 16–19, 30

Shi'a and Sunni split in, 8, 16–18, 30, 34, 54, 88
spread of, 13, 29–30, 34, 35–36, 38–39
and terrorism, 90–91
timeline of, 98–101
values of, 71–91
and women's rights, 76–78
worship practices in, 57–60, 62–69
    See also Muhammad; Qur'an
Islamic Jihad, 90
Islamic Society, 88
Islamism, 88–91
Isma'il (Ishmael), 62, 65, 67, *68*

Jerusalem, *35*, 37, 54, 67
Jibreel (Gabriel), 22
jihad, 70, 85–87, 90
Judaism, 15, 22, 23, 29–30, 92, 94, 95

Ka'bah, 56, *66*, 67, *68*, 69
Kadijah (wife of Muhammad), 24, *25*, 28, 74
Kharijis, 33
Khomeini, Ayatollah, 88

Lailat-ul-Barat (Night of Forgiveness), 55, 96
Lailat-ul-Isra'wal Miraj (Night Journey), 54–55, 96
Lailat-ul-Qadr (Night of Power), 55, 96
Libya, 15, 34, *89*

Malaysia, *73, 76*, 90
marriage and family life, 72–76, 77, 78–79
masjid. *See* mosques
Maulid ul Nabi, 54, 96
Mecca, Saudi Arabia, *6*, 21, 22, 24, 27, 38, 49, 54, 95

and pilgrimages, 40, 42, 43, 56,
   62–64, 67, 69
medical technology, 83–84
Medina, Saudi Arabia, 24, 27, 28,
   29, 35, 40, 43, 49, 67
Mongol invasion, 37–38, 39
months. *See* calendar, Islamic
mosques, *11, 35, 36*, 51, 56, 60, *61*
   Great Mosque (Mecca), 66, 67
Muawiya (caliph), 31, *32*, 33, 34
Muhammad, 8, 9, *25, 26*, 40, *48,
   53*, 54, 74, 81, 82, 87
   death and burial of, 27–28, *29*,
      43, 67
   and the Hadith, 20
   and history of Islam, 13, 21–22,
      23, 24, 27–28
   life of, 21–22, 24, 27, 43, 49,
      62, 67, 69
   Night Journey of, 54–55
   successors of, 17–18, 28–35
   and the Sunnah, 70, 71–72
   See also Islam
Musa (Moses), 23
Muslim Brotherhood, 88
Muslims. *See* Islam

Nuh (Noah), 23

Ottoman Empire, *38*, 39

Pakistan, 13, *14, 17*, 77
Palestine, *86*, 90
pilgrimage, 40, 42, 60, 62–67
Hajj, 40, 42, 50, 52, 56, 62–67, 69
polygamy, 74, *75*
prayers (salah), 40, *41*, 42, 56, 57,
   58–60
prophets, 8, 10, 23

Qur'an, 8, 12, 15, 23, *31*, 43, 46,
   86–87, 95
   first compilation of the, 30

learning by heart, *16*, 27
and the revelations of
   Muhammad, 22, 23, 43, 55,
   71
and Shari'ah, 70, 72, 75
and values of Islam, 70, 77,
   78–81, 82, 83
See also Islam

Ramadan, 40, 42, 43, *44*, 51–52,
   55, 96
research projects, 19, 39, 55, 91
rituals, 41, 45–47

sacrifices, animal, 45, *50*, 52, 65,
   85, *96*
salah. *See* prayers (salah)
sanctity of life, 81–83, 85
Saudi Arabia, 77, *79, 89*, 95
   Medina, 24, 27, 28, *29*, 35, 40,
      43, 49, 67
   pilgrimages to, 40, 42, 43, 56,
      62–64, 67, 69
   See also Mecca, Saudi Arabia
sawm. *See* fasting (sawm)
Shahadah, 10, 42
Shari'ah, 70, 72, 75
Shi'a Islam, 8, 16–18, 30, 34, 54, 88
   See also Islam
Spain, 34, 37
Sufism, 18, 19
Sunnah, 70, 71–72
Sunni Islam, 8, 16–18
   See also Islam
Syria, 29, 31, 34, 35

Talib, Ali ibn Abi. *See* Ali (Ali ibn
   Abi Talib)
terrorism, 90–91
Turkey, *14*, 37, 39, 77, 90

Umar (caliph), 28–29, 30
Umayyad dynasty, 33, 34–35, 36

Uthman (caliph), 30

values, Muslim, 71–72
    and dietary restrictions, 84–85
    and fundamentalism, 70, 87–90
    marriage and family life, 72–76,
        77, 78–79
    and medical technology, 83–84
    and prohibited vices, 79–81
    the sanctity of life, 81–83, 85
    and women's rights, 76–78
    See also Islam
vices, prohibited, 79–81

washing (worship practice), 57–58,
    60, *68*
women's rights, 76–78

Yazid (son of Muawiya), 33

Zaidis (sect), 19
zakah (charity), 40, 42, 44–45, 52

About the Author

Michael Ashkar is a graduate of the University of Michigan. This is his first book for young people.